# Bruised but Unbroken

**Revised**

*poems & stories*

CHERYL ANTAO-XAVIER

# Bruised but unbroken *revised*

by Cheryl Antao-Xavier

*published by:* In Our Words Inc. / inourwords.ca
*designed by:* Shirley Aguinaldo
*cover image:* Dreamstime.com
*inside images:* Dreamstime.com/Shutterstock.com
123RF.com/Pixabay.com
*editors:* I.B. Iskov/Brandon Pitts
*author photo:* Lisa Mininni / lisaphoto.ca

First printing, April 2011
Revised edition, April 2017

Library and Archives Canada Cataloguing in Publication
Antao-Xavier, Cheryl, author
Bruised but unbroken / Cheryl Antao-Xavier. -- Revised edition.
Poems and short stories.
Issued in print and electronic formats.
ISBN 978-1-926926-78-0 (softcover).--ISBN 978-1-926926-79-7 (PDF)
I. Title.

PS8601.N58B78 2016 C811'.6 C2016-908048-X C2016-908049-8

# Dedication

To my *Sisters* = my inspiration

*Nora*: who finds her paths in life

*Agnes*: whose faith and support carries us all

*Sandra*: who lived her dreams

# Contents

A Prayer....................................7
Bruised but Unbroken............9
Teaching Moments................10
Promise of Spring..................11
Outside Face...........................12
Hate Words............................13
The Cup.................................14
Memories of Light.................15
Priorities................................16
Fear.........................................17
Serenity in the Moment........18
Food for Thought..................19
Dining in the Moment..........20
Changing Kismet...................21
Old Baggage...........................22
No Replicas of this, Please...23
Domination............................24
In the Bell Tower...................25
Enough...................................26
Old Issues came to Visit.......27
Reckoning..............................28
Shells.......................................29
Unhealed Wounds................30
Band Apart.............................31
No Roses, Just Dandelions...33
You are Gone.........................34
The New Canada..................35

## On Writing

Creative Misgivings.............37
Words of Wisdom.................38
Shifting Mood........................39
No Dreams.............................40
Words of Love.......................41
The Power of Poetry.............42
Discounted Dreams..............43
Tired Muse.............................44
Seeking New Spheres...........45
Look with Kind Eyes............47
A Memoir...............................48
Uneasy Peace........................49

## On War and Peace

Unknown Soldier ..................51
On Both Sides ........................52
To a Refugee...........................53
The Sounds of War................54
Save Your Tears.....................55
Faith Revisited.......................56
Thank You, Canada .............57
By Life's Way .........................59
The Banyan Tree....................61
Monsoon Tears ......................62
World of Waste......................63
Under the Maple Tree ..........64
Planting anew ........................65
Petal Perfect ...........................66
Dancing Daisies.....................67
Sukoon*..................................69

## Mind Shift

Mind Shift..............................71
Rise Up! Rise Above! ............73
Cat Inspiration.......................75
Living Moments ....................76
Utopian Moments .................77

## Vignettes of Life

Lest I Forget ...........................79
Going Home...........................80
Parenting Revised .................81
For Bradley.............................82
Toppling of an Idol ...............83
My Way ..................................84
Lesson From Big Mama........85
Then and Now.......................86
The Procedure........................87
Box of Treasures ....................88
Girl..........................................89
Soul Sister ...............................90
I am Home..............................91
I Love Canada, Because........93
Small Iniquity ........................94
The Little Red Streamer........95
A Prayer.................................96
Reviews for 'Bruised but
Unbroken'..............................97

# A Prayer...

Dear Lord,

Be the beacon that lights me
through the mists of indecision.
May my vision widen
beyond all perils, real or imagined
to encompass the universe.

Be the light that guides my work
and all that I do
with a steady hand
to stay on purpose
and keep the course
to the harbour of all good.

Keep Spirit alive
in the bruised,
so they rise out of misfortune
healed and unbroken.

*A triumph of spirit is to continue to grow*
*even in the most arid of plains.*
*To hope and pray for rain,*
*yet whether or not it comes,*
*to live each moment.*

# Bruised but Unbroken

Soil splits and sprouts emerge.
Parched land offers little hope,
yet tiny tentacles of life
thrust towards the sky
praying for blessings to shower
on thirsting roots.

Spirit endures through tribulation
more resilient
rekindling hope.

In there lies survival.
Life sprouts anew.

Few reach maturity unscathed by life.
To endure and to survive
is to have the power to say
'I am bruised but unbroken.'

## Teaching Moments

Will I forever be watching for
clouds to darken my horizons
and miss the flowers at my feet
picked by small, loving hands.

Innocent eyes watch me
tiny feet shuffle in my footsteps.
My every mood caught and mirrored
with frightening clarity
forcing me
to weather storms
and look for rainbows.

## haiku

deep in the ocean
stirs a raging force unseen
a tsunami birth

# Promise of Spring

Adversity strikes hard
at pride and confidence
leaving in its wake
stumped prospects
bruised egos and devastated dreams.

Spirit remains unbroken
gleaning wisdom from harsh times
expecting the cycle of life
to unfurl new promises in spring.

I behold the chance at renewal
to push past severed trunks and
truncated branches
to thrive fresh and hopeful
with vision and purpose
clear and strong.

# Outside Face

Bruised by life
scars don't show.

A comb calms the disarray
a dash of colour
eyeshadow to blot the real.

Outside face
ready to meet the world
a smile hides
lessons learned
wisdom earned.

# haiku

careless words pierce deep
deadliest of all weapons
wounds forever raw

# Hate Words

Slurs hit the airwaves
as shrapnel in the inner ear
piercing the psyche
feeding indelible stereotypes of prejudice.

Slurs impact with the weight of
age-old connotations
piercing soul-deep
splitting open generational wounds
baring festering hatreds,
with reminders that a time of
bigotry        brutality        ignorance
lurks below the surface of civility.

Slurs hurled to demean
spatter indiscriminately
and smear us all.

# The Cup

I did not mean so much to you
as you did to me.

You were gone before the sun was up
and I washed your cup
put it away on the shelf
never thinking that last trace
of your lips
on the rim of my faded china
would be all that I'd have left
to remember you by.

You never thought to leave
anything more.

Still I remember you
every time
I look at that cup
sitting on that shelf
with never a speck of dust on it.

# Memories of Light

Sun-dappled shadows
formed from luxuriant bougainvillea
sprawled over
the wrought iron gates of home.

Late afternoon sunshine
welcomed with drawn curtains
shone on the tea table
fond memory of home.

Sunset through stained glass
lit up polished pews
imbued an air of sanctity
to the memory of evensong.

Soft sunshine and mellow afternoons
spark nostalgic moments.
Peace and tranquility
ease gently on my mind.

# Priorities

The tide will come in and ebb once more.
Spectacular sunrises and sunsets
the northern lights
will delight
in other times.

Now
I will cherish you
and my time with you.

There is the chance
that tomorrow
you may not be here.

# haiku

i shall pour my heart
in words of poems and song
seeing what happens

# Fear

Fear itches under my skin
forcing attention
till I pick at it
even though I promised myself
I would never again
allow fear to take control.

Wounds of the past must heal
with only scars
faint reminders
to never again cede power
to another
to wield against me.

I can rise above my fears.
I have healed.
I am strong again.

# Serenity in the Moment

Snowflakes alight soundlessly on glass.
I watch as my world is draped
in pristine, virginal white.
Serenity of the moment enters my soul.

I am cocooned in my car
with the doors locked
parked on the driveway
looking at the house where I live.
I feel safe
for now.

# haiku

roses and jasmine
permeate the mourning soul
scents of love and death

# Food for Thought

Years of vanity-driven diets
built up pounds of discontent
stringing unwanted connotations of foreboding
around the word 'food.'

The specter of parsimony looms
across the table of plenty
equating good taste and satiety
with perceptions of excess and gluttony.

Even before the feast has begun
guilt tempers temptation
turning good wine and food
into sour grapes and sawdust.

# haiku

if food be god's love
summer fruit fresh off the tree
taste of the divine

# Dining in the Moment

A feast for the soul
and triumph of the spirit
is to serve leftovers
with your best linen, crystal and china
raising a flute of sparkling water
in a toast to the good life.

# haiku

each day moves forward
takes me one step from the past
let me live today

# Changing Kismet

Wordless cries
resonate in silence
like dust motes
suspended in sunbeams
there—but—not there
seen only when the light
shines through the darkness.

In this land—in this place of hope—
there is shelter from the darkness
for those who dare to
push back the bolts of silence
walk into the light
and redefine Kismet.

# haiku

dewdrops or teardrops
the poet's eye sees much more
beauty reflected

# Old Baggage

From one home to the next
from one land to the other
across the sea and over land
to newer and better
they drag mountains of baggage
old worn-out customs
ancient prejudices
unpack and stash away
in new cupboards.

Why?
To surround themselves
with all that they ran away from?

# haiku

spring's brushstrokes create
snowy white masterpieces
cherry blossom blooms

# No Replicas of this, Please

When we cross oceans and space
to seek new lands
and create new homes

let it not be
in order to create
more of what we have already.

No more replicas of this, please.

# haiku

spring oleander
dies early in april frost
hope is laid to rest

# Domination

She sees her son bullying his sister.
He hits her.
He takes her toy.

She sees no need to intervene.
Culture plays out in culture-bound lives.

"Mama, tell him to leave me alone."

"*Beta*!" the rebuke cuts through the present
echoes into the future
of her son
and her daughter.

*Author's note: beta means 'son'*

# In the Bell Tower

No wedding bells ring
for two
who defied God's ... nay, man's rule
that forbids uniting of
creatures of the same sex.

Joy and pride ring out.

The silence is deafening in the bell tower.

# haiku

harsh light blurs vision
true pathways to the future
right has no left turn

# Enough

Time to cut
the invisible umbilical cord
and apron strings.
Take off that band
that last sign of a failed commitment.

Time
for the child
the parent
the spouse
to say enough is enough.

I need to put some distance
between us
if I am to recover
a sense of myself.

# Old Issues came to Visit

Negativity blew through my front door
left an aura on the sofa
in the guest room
in my fridge.
Old resentments
with severed ties
were gifted to me
for my new life.

I silently toss them
rid all traces
of unwanted reminders
of old issues
from my new life.

I have learned to say
with conviction
the next time old issues
want to visit
sorry, I won't be here.

# Reckoning

Hapless, spineless
for letting you hit me
and get away with a 'sorry'
such wounds don't heal easily.

You learned that day
that you could do it again
and I would just take it and take it.
Always.

But the day came
when the screaming in my head
surged through
a vengeful hand.

I did unto you
what you did
unto me.
Day of reckoning.

# Shells

Sheltered lives
beached, high and dry
snatched, swept away
on raging tides.

Quashed lives
sucked out
hollowed sonorous
sounds of the deep.

Crusty walls
hardened by tribulation
smashed on rocks.
The wreckage washed ashore.

Naked, bleached
shattered shells
vestiges of past lives.

# Unhealed Wounds

Sharp-tongued weapons
scar deeply.

Too often mean words
overwhelm the meek
pulling them back to the line
of mediocrity.

Truth is vanquished
and the righteous lose their way.
Justice conspires
to hurt the hands that hurt.
Fate reaches out to salve
unhealed wounds.

# haiku

dying sun laments
mourns in darkness of the night
dawn brings some relief

# Band Apart

Do not expect me
to be part of your identity
as I do not identify you
with who or what I am.

That little band we exchanged
in innocence
grew to be a noose.
You and I so individual
expected to couple on everything.

I am me
and you are you
and let's just stay that way.
Never mind the tradition
wrapped around that little band.

Let it lie upon the dresser
it's still a pretty trinket
we gave each other.

# In the Sunset Years

Looking at sunsets on the horizon,
I do not pine for sunshine
and cloudless skies.

I do not wish for applause
nor fear condescension.

My eyes hunger for
love and gratitude
every day
and all surprises
          good or bad.

In the sunset years
I see my life's moments
          aglow.

## No Roses, Just Dandelions

Over the years, the cares
faded the blush from this cheek
stole the bloom from this rose.
Been awhile since the roses came.
No Valentines, no anniversary bouquet.
Just a clutch of dandelions
from her gap-toothed beau.

His love is sure
and she has learned
to look no further.

## haiku

covet from afar
across water lily blooms
beauty beyond reach

# You are Gone

You are gone
and I am not as bereft of joy
as I think I should be.

The silence is peaceful,
freedom a welcome release.

This testimony is pinned
to a diamond-studded sky
as proof of a dimmed star
that dared come back to shine.

You are gone
and I have an eagerness
to fly somewhere,
anywhere.

# The New Canada

Gradually old ingrained notions
of *us* and *them* slough off as
dead scales of prejudice
on all sides—
grows new skin
from generation to generation.

Social fabric unravels
and is rewoven with fingers of benevolence
stretching across high stakes of patriotism
standing tall
united with common values
endured and enhanced
Canadian ideals.

The old Canada.
The new Canada.

# On Writing

*I feel the gratitude for tranquil moments*

# Creative Misgivings

Fresh off the press
misgivings set in.

Words rise off the printed page
suddenly naked in banality.

Flawed visionary or posturing fool?

The reality of this book
joins the multitude of tomes
lining dusty shelves
disintegrating in landfills
lost in the Amazonian highways of anonymity.

Misgivings stymie inspiration.

If I am ever to write
I must stand behind my words
proud of raising my voice
to leave a legacy in print.

# Words of Wisdom

Words of wisdom
penned with diligence.
Just words
written and rewritten
different ways.
A writer's legacy
inspires for years to come.

Old wisdom gleaned.

Once the ink dries
the legend is entombed.

The writer sighs,
picks up the pen
returns to diligence.

# haiku

angels whisper soft
in gentle soulful urgings
to the inner self

# Shifting Mood

When negativity leads my pencil
verse blackens,
the mood darkens.

I gaze upon the tranquility of my haven.
I hear ripples of clear water.
Bird calls evoke reminisces of nature retreats.
I hear distant oddly-soothing sounds
of rail hydraulics, prompting
memories of comings and goings,
good times tempered by sad times.

I feel the gratitude for tranquil moments.

I chase away black verse
shifting mood,
mindset and vision,
language and idiom
to reflect on happier times
now.

# No Dreams

What happens when you achieve the dream
and reach for the next one
only to find
you have lost interest in dreams?

You strayed beyond the limits
of intent, of passion.
Suddenly the big dreamer
you once were
feels lost in the great void
of the unappreciated.

You wander aimlessly along trodden paths
of a life that is no longer recognizable.

What happens when dreamers
dream no more?

# Words of Love

I cannot speak words of love
for they were never spoken to me.
I love not the way lovers do
for I was never taught that lesson.

I will not read you the words of others
from poems and famous love letters.
Those words though fine and fancy
sound false upon my tongue.

I cannot write what's in my heart
for I lack the poet's lexis.
I speak in the silence of devotion
in a language that needs no words.

# haiku

spirits speak softly
whispering through the ages
warning those who heed

## The Power of Poetry

After the reading ends
the poet walks away
oblivious of the pain inflicted
emotions unleashed
scabs scraped off
old forgotten wounds
bleeding afresh
fevered eyes stung by hot tears
quivering lips, stony stares
wooden jaws

souls bared
by the unwitting power
of a poet who bears witness
to his own heartbreak.

## haiku

dreams flit on light wings
skimming surfaces of life
tease reality

# Discounted Dreams

The lines between others' dreams for me
and my dreams
somehow got blurred in the mad rush
to do  to be  to achieve.

Suddenly, I see

how I perpetuate the vicious cycle
blurring the lines of want and need
dreams and shams
create a surreal life of fuzzy ideals.
Allow my vision to be discounted as
a pipe dream.
Idle indulgence.
Nonsense.
Mid-life crises.

It's not easy to dismount
from this vicious cycle
and retrieve old dreams.

Gotta ride on.
No time for dreams.

## Tired Muse

Lovelorn declarations
drip cloyingly on my restless brain
sounding like
hackneyed lies.

Words of heart-break
make great titles
for love-gone-wrong stories.
But can my muse
rise from stymieing apathy and
come up with anything
to meet the expectation
of high drama?

## haiku

sparkling crystal heart
shatters into smithereens
spirit perishes

# Seeking New Spheres

The published poet
erupts on the literary scene
ego at an all-time high.
Bouncing on sensitive toes
often linked to petty minds,
seeing not the merit in the work,
        the uniqueness in vision, in voice, in style,
but the poet -- someone they know.
Or think they know.
So they prick at the ego -- to deflate it
just because they can.

The jokes begin
"It sounds nice…but"
        This from one who never reads.
"Did you really write that?"
        This from one who has no muse.
"But why did you publish your book?"
        *This* from one who has no ambition.

The published poet -- wiser
seeks new spheres
in readers, writers and dreamers.

# Elegy for a Creative Soul

*For BP*

The light in your eyes
died along with your poetry.
Creative inspiration vanquished
for mundane profit
blinding vision to the beauty in life.

Who noticed the silence
felt the emptiness
saw the darkness
in your eyes?
The loss is ours as well as yours.

Who – from a place of power
will pause in their own doings
to stoke the fire
of inspiration and passion
rekindle hope
before we are buried
in the ashes of creative souls?

# Look with Kind Eyes

When I stand up for what I believe in
and rock the boat against the tide
will you applaud
even if you disagree
even if you fear that
I'm not quite mainstream?
Will you still look upon me with kind eyes?

When I pour my heart
and soul into my creations
shade them with exotic colours
and hold them up with pride
and place them next to your creations
will you look at them with an open mind
and see the beauty?
Will you look upon them with kind eyes?

When I step out of the margins
and venture along paths
that you walk so confidently
will you make way for me
or pretend you don't see me?
Will you watch passively
while I'm denigrated to the sidelines?
Will you look at me with kind eyes?

# A Memoir

On blank pages, I wrote my story
from sheltered life to the real world
of rigid values tempering.
Life events then and now
reflected in the writing.
I see what was meant to be.

In my diary, I wrote
of tormenters who changed my life
pushed me where I would not have gone
of demons that lurk unresolved
like burrs in my psyche.

To write of them was to see
how a foe can be a friend
and burrs and demons cannot hurt
if I have the will to remove them.

Freedom from the past
clarity of perception
rise off the pages of
a memoir.

# Uneasy Peace

The sounds of murder and mayhem resonate
through the house.
The peace of evening
is shattered by cries of injustice
senseless violence
expletive-peppered language.

My gut clenches involuntarily.
Fear tightens its grip on fragile nerves.
Visions of brutality sear into memory.

A pair of headphones
clamped on the offender's head
returns us to a quiet, but
uneasy peace.

# haiku

shalom—term for peace
gentle on the fevered mind
a Hebrew mantra

# On war and peace

*Justice and freedom*
*often come at a costly price.*

# Unknown Soldier

Justice and freedom
often come at a costly price.
Precious lives lost for a nation's triumph
are honoured in salute and prayer.

In the shadows of anonymity
faceless heroes stand tall.
History remembers the unnamed
once loved by a few
now celebrated by a nation.

# haiku

whispers in the wind
fields of swaying blood poppies
promise to keep faith

# On Both Sides

The soldiers of the light brigade
marched to a sure death.
Duty triumphed over rationality
for warriors and power mongers
on both sides of the battle lines.

Every man standing questioned not
the wisdom of war called by some
and waged in the name of all
with innocent lives in the line of fire
on both sides of the battle lines.

Duty, honour, nation, freedom
and the powerful word patriotism,
quell dissention. Justify united fronts,
unmarked graves and body bags
on both sides of the battle lines.

But on the homefront
the questions lurk. Reasons fade as
countless connected lives
stand on the shoulders of soldiers
on both sides of the battle lines.

# To a Refugee

Tell me not your tales of woe
I have heard them all before
they tell of other distant worlds
far from the safety of my home.

Easy to deliberate
how the tyranny of a few
could annihilate the lives of so many.
I watch from afar
as injustices rage across continents
touching all people
again and again
as history repeats itself
indifferent to race or creed.

Flipping from channel to channel
surfing for nonviolence
I try to avoid the reality of brutality
with a flick of the remote.

Tell me not your tales of woe
for I have heard them all before
tell me instead how I can help
to give you back some sense of home.

# The Sounds of War

The banshee wails of wartime sirens.
Screeching jets breaking sound barriers.
The whistle of raining bombs.
Staccato thud of ground fire.

These are the sounds of war.

Quaking heartbeats and blind terror
of exploding worlds -- lives
of mothers, sisters, daughters, the aged
guarding a defenseless home front.

These are the realities of war.

The sounds of war
once heard
the realities of war
once felt
forever echo.

# Save Your Tears

Save your tears for them
who tie yellow ribbons to trees
tuck baby booties in army fatigues
slip their pictures into wallets
watch alone baby's first steps
explain the absences with fake smiles
and sleep alone at night.

Save your tears for them
who make overseas calls with anticipation
but dread sombre official calls
who accept the flag with trembling hands
pick up the pieces of shattered goals
put them back together
honour the missing place at the dining table
and lament their loss for years and years
after the spotlight dies.

Save your tears
for our living heroes
who share
in that ultimate sacrifice.

# Faith Revisited

*Yahweh! Jehovah! God! Allah!*
His words, misconstrued in the minds of man
spewed off pulpits and blasted from minarets
upon proselytized non-thinkers
who ingest the vomit of sickly minds
and regurgitate it through generations
each espousing a superiority over others
a chosen race, with a mission to save the world.
And the cacophony of colliding dogma
echoes across nations and over bloodied battlefields
dividing mankind along spurious fault lines
indoctrinating male superiority and female inferiority
wielding holy books like sacred weapons
ascribing man's convoluted interpretations of
an angry, vengeful god.

If sacred texts are gleaned for the spirit of goodwill
if holy wars are denounced as unholy
if organized religion is stripped of dissention
would the faithful still be faithful
would they still come
to a common altar and proclaim:
*My God! Ya Allah! Jehovah! Yahweh!?*

# Thank You, Canada

for the pride in our banner
respected worldwide

for the right to live in a land
where equality and freedom
are core values

for a life of security
peace and justice.

Thank you, Canada
for being the voice of reason
persevering through the rhetoric
for open borders
and peopling the land
with a rich and healthy diversity.

Thank you, Canada.

*Streams flow to the sea,*
*gurgling brooks, raging rivers,*
*same water, changed forever*
*by life's way*

# By Life's Way

Storms pass
gloomy skies lighten up
earth thrives refreshed.

An analogy for life.

Burdens of yesterday
lighten with time
trials in resilience.

Streams flow to the sea
gurgling brooks, raging rivers
same water, changed forever
by life's way.

Youth to old age,
what a journey!
Same soul, changed forever
by life's way…

*Nature's hand soared wildly*
*creating a mammoth masterpiece.*
*A powerful patriarch,*
*the giant banyan tree.*

# The Banyan Tree

Four generations nestled
in arms like sturdy pillars.
Nature's hand soared wildly
creating a mammoth masterpiece.
A powerful patriarch,
the giant banyan tree.

One by one its siblings fell
to make way for urban sprawl.
The banyan tree was the last to go,
a defiant spectre to the end.
They razed it and built over
the grave of the banyan tree.

Ghostly roots lay there to haunt
in land never ceded,
from cracks in the ground tentacles arose
reaching beyond the concrete tomb,
reminders of a life that once existed
before Nature lost to man's creations,
relentlessly smothered,
in the wake of his pollution,
before the clamour of city life drowned
the sounds of gently rustling leaves,
and the eerie blaze of neon lights
doused the shades of the banyan tree.

# Monsoon Tears

Sheets of rain like bitter tears
sting an upturned face.

The monsoons pass
dark clouds rumble off.

A rainbow faint
but undeniably
points the way forward
across to new horizons.

The journey continues…

# haiku

monsoon rain falls soft
icy shards in the winter
warm summer showers

# World of Waste

Plastic islands float in the Pacific.

The grace of a lone canoe
as a scavenger looks for treasure
in a sea of debris.

Mounds of green grass
undulate as far as the eye can see.
Toxic grounds lie over graves of trash.

A halo of pollution crowns Mother Earth.
Slow strangulation of all living things.
Each day brings new fears for our ecosphere
constantly littering my brain.

# haiku

hope darkened by cloud
know the sun will rise again
wait for the clearing

# Under the Maple Tree

Nature creates a little magic
in every single leaf
a microcosmic wonder
adorns trees in great diversity
in autumn they drop in glory
to scatter and come together
in multi-coloured magnificence
under the maple tree.

# haiku

beauty comes alive
in the strewn lines of stone
shades of the mosaic

# Planting anew

This Spring
I will plough deep
rooting out the rot
that lurks beneath
the façade of propriety.

Planting new seeds
in fruitful soil
to burgeon wholesome
expectant bounty
bursting with goodness
when the time comes to reap.

This Spring
I will clean deep
pruning all I need
keeping only what matches
the outer persona
with the ideals in my head.

This Spring
there will be a fresh beginning.

# Petal Perfect

The perfect symmetrical flower
bright, cheerful yellow
sprouts in the shadow of rock
in a vast chasm of boulders.

No paths lead here
no trekker, no naturalist, no poet
ever stopped by to ponder on its hardiness
and be inspired by its petal-perfect beauty.

Never appreciated
not even by the mountain goat
that snapped it up
chomped on it twice
and swallowed it semi-whole.

# haiku

tulip unravels
behold its time of glory
the first petal falls

## Dancing Daisies

Daisies in the field
wither under harsh sun

then buried in snowy shrouds.
Spring again year after year
to fill the fields
with dancing daisies.

## haiku

bud unfurls shyly
beauty reaches for the sky
exhilarated

*I inhale serenity*
*feel, imbibe*
*sukoon*

# Sukoon*

When life stretches in monotony
and stress oppresses

I escape to where cool waters flow
and lush green soothes.

I inhale serenity.
Feel, imbibe

sukoon.

**Sukoon is the Urdu word for tranquility*

# Mind Shift

HEAVY REJECTED DISTURBING COMFORT HEAVENLY VICTORIOUS
SHAMEFUL DEFEATED HATE SUPERIOR VISIBLE BRIGHT
REWARDING ACCEPTED POSITIVE EASY
NAUGHTY DISCOMFORT DIFFICULT LIKE STRONG
DARK FALSE STRESSED WRONG INCLUDED RELAXED PEACEFUL
HELLISH HATE WEAK WORSE FAILURE GOOD TRUE PROUD
WEAK DEAD UNSAFE BETTER
INFERIOR IRRITATING LESS NICE RIGHT EASY
EVIL INVISIBLE UNSAFE LIGHT SUCCESSFUL
DEAD NEGATIVE EXCLUDED HEAVY PLEASANT STRONG MORE
REPULSIVE WORSE ALIVE
WRONG HELLISH PUNISHING FAILURE ATTRACTIVE GOOD
WORTHLESS SHAMEFUL VALUABLE TRUE
EVIL DARK LESS SAFE VICTORIOUS
Follow Hold Pause Allow Be with Listen
Thank Greet Breathe
Accept Sense Trust Be with
Feel Open Breathe Slow down Pause
Let go Listen Accept Reflect
Trust Observe Notice Hold Greet Invite
Open Sense Trust Release Attend Admit
Acknowledge Attend Appreciate Feel
Embrace Welcome Observe Notice
Feel Follow
Receive Accept Feel Greet Reflect
Sense Welcome Feel Appreciate Invite

# Mind Shift

Joy = loss
loss = gain
gain = failure
failure = stress
stress = negativity
negativity = depression.

Mind shift.

Depression = contemplation
contemplation = gratitude
gratitude = possibility
possibility = positivity
positivity = contentment
contentment = joy.

release
SUN peace dance
good save
friendship burning fruits help
worry jovial
fist jealousy great well balance
shadow understanding honest felt
apart ugly death
miserable desperate COLD QUALITY music
butterfly up
drowning welcome open
cut stress rape ANGER LOVE cute
curse fear There lonely devil fresh
money
cheat HUNGER is always bleed water nurtured timeless
meditation
empty bad loss plus leisure Good
a dark fury
humiliation ill BROKEN compassion joy hug
gossip rotten breeze
unfair tears sausage weak DREAM
HATE bondage dewdrop
whining posesivity colors magic bliss
disappointment sing
grumpy lust astral beautiful
cry agony gorgeous smile humble simple prayer
selfish sick catchy clean harmony
BEAT
sadness anxiety FULL possibility neat adorable meadow
closed filthy burning life fit of warm
perverted miracle angel
minus WRONG bounce heart change fair
nice
wicked force RUN! cherish right rainbow
deadline kill fall together light
nightmare kind satisfied lovely
chaos phobia noise freedom
denial suicide
bully GOD flowers
hollow GREED tears healthy
bad shattered ignore
harm time poverty ugly

# Rise Up! Rise Above!

The journey to a Life of Possibility
begins with promise.
Plans take flight,
the road opens, the universe beckons
and then life happens.

Out of dark shadows come the denigrators
the stealers of vision.
Anchors that dredge the past
dragging old issues into the present
weighting the now,
tarnishing the tomorrows
with tainted visions of diminished dreams,
lowered expectations.

Rise above!

Rise above fissures in the road
dug into ever-widening chasms by naysayers
who create unsurpassable rifts
in the pathways of true creators,
who attempt to purloin
the visions of dreamers.

Rise up, rise above!

*Nestled in home comfort:*
*a good book, a steaming beverage*
*good company at a good distance.*
*This is my Utopia.*

# Cat Inspiration

My neighbour's cat appears at the usual hour,
jumps off the low dividing wall
and moseys across our front yard
to hop on the bonnet of my car,
sprawl languidly, stretching both paws
as far as they will go.

In mid-stretch, she rolls onto her other side
to catch every last ray of late afternoon sun
swatting at an insect, watching its flight,
keening at a dog's bark in the distance.
Ears twitch like antennae
as her mistress calls out to her
*Binchy! Binchy!*
Binchy blinks and looks unconcerned,
curls up and closes her eyes.

I turn my own eyes back
to the book I'm reading on meditation.
The chapter is 'Living in the Moment.'
I've just got the gist of it
from my neighbour's cat.

# Living Moments

There's my neighbour's cat again.
What'll she teach me this time?
I lay down my book to watch
her amble across our driveway
pausing to inspect random objects,
batting lightly at each with an inquisitive paw.

I recall tranquil moments years ago
when I wandered around our yard
in the afternoon sunshine
picking up stones and random things,
creating stories around them
as a child.

I watch from the window
wishing I could ease once more into a
pure     carefree     let-it-be existence
without a twinge of guilt
and be at ease in the moment.

## Utopian Moments

Beautiful wintery scene
snow-covered world outside my window
nestled in home comfort:
a good book, a steaming beverage
good company at a good distance.

This is my Utopia.

## haiku

snowcaps start to melt
quietly through the balmy night
await the deluge

# vignettes of Life

# Lest I Forget

Lest I forget
the many hands that raised me,
lifted me when I needed lifting,
taught me hard lessons in kind ways
and sometimes in harsh ways,
influences that continue
into the present and the future.

Lest I forget
to be grateful for them.

I look back on the vibrant fields of life
dimming in fading memory.

Lest I forget
the times, the places, the people
that made my defining moments.

# Going Home

What would you do if we come home?
Will you be by the garden wall
peering past the bougainvillea
watching for the first sight of us?
And when you see us coming,
will you hurry indoors
to put the water on to boil
for a nice cup of tea?
Will you get busy making vermicelli,
suji halwa or everyone's favourite
green dal with coconut and Goa jaggery?
Or slice open freshly-delivered karak rotis
and smother each half with a pat of butter,
homemade mulberry jam
and a dollop of thick cream,
skimmed off home-pasteurized milk?

If we knew you were waiting,
we would leave everything
and come home.

# Parenting Revised

He walks out the door,
18 years of over-confidence belied
in the nonchalance of his slouch.

I question or pry, he says,
*where are you off to?*
*Who with?*
*Do you know what curfew means?*

Seeking to forestall mishaps,
getting nowhere close to the attention
my mother received
when instilling the fear of God and man,
sending her daughters off into life,
quiet, reserved, cautious.
She forewarned of vices that stalk virtue.
It was her way of looking out for us.

Not wanting to hold him back,
I revise parenting.

He walks out the door,
teenage eagerness ready to experiment
with vice and virtue
to decide for himself wrong and right.
My heart follows him with a blessing.

# For Bradley

Bradley
I draw out your memory
from the dark shadows of my heart
bathe it once more
in the light of a mother's love
inhale your baby scent
remembered as is
your soft cooing in my ear.

I get out your pictures
so few, so few
had we but known
you'd leave so soon
I'd have taken so many snapshots
as to wallpaper the rest of our lives
with your image
so no one will ever forget
that you lived
that you are always a part of us.

# Toppling of an Idol

I came to hear him read
anticipation seeped through pores.
Chill in the air of eager expectations.
My ears strained to catch the first hint
of his presence at the podium.
Over the heads of distraction
I craned to glimpse my idol
prepared to be transported
mesmerized by every word.
Pure gold
words of a master.
His six volumes
lined the top shelf of my prized collection
never lent out.

He stooped like one defeated.
Disillusionment was in his eyes,
his voice shaded the profundity of his vision.
His words somehow seemed leaden.

Disenchanted, I left.

# My Way

*For Cynthia*

I have an enduring memory of you
dressed to the nines
sashaying down your own path
with a bravado so fragile
only a few sensed.
Never doubted that the path
of the straight and narrow
was never paved for you.

You trampled across the lines of propriety
soared over boundaries of inhibitions.
You broke through the bubble
of cultural claustrophobia,
shrugged off convention
revealed the rebel
bold, beautiful, totally unrepentant
danced on tabletops, belted out
Old Blue Eyes' swan song
"I did it my way."

# Lesson From Big Mama

Yes, funny boy, here I come
all 350 pounds of beautiful me.
Am I in your way, boy?
Get used to it
for I ain't goin' away,
jus' cuz the sight o' me offends you.
I ain't gonna hide
cuz I make you uncomfortable.
If you don't like what you see
no one's askin' you to look at me.
Now I don't give a hoot
for the likes o' you,
so don't be tickin' me off, sonny,
cuz I may jus forget the manners
ma mama taught me
and set these fabulous curves
down upon your smartass face
and then…

… never mind,
let's not spoil the lesson.
Just give me a reason
to teach you better.

# Then and Now

*For LP*

Her voice is the same.
She has the same last name
but the woman I now see
is a whole lot different from
the sassy rebel
I knew three decades ago.
I put the faded picture on the table
of the two of us, arms around each other
laughing blissfully,
so carefree, so ambitious,
so long ago.

We look across into each other's eyes.
The reminiscing is shadowed
and we smile ruefully.
Both thinking, if we could only go back in time.
Many mistakes would not have been made.

# The Procedure

*For P*

You grab the doctor's hand
clinging, pleading
*Please, please make me not have more.*
"It's against the law," she says.
*Never mind, you beseech. No one will know.*
"Speak to your husband."
*He is a man. He doesn't understand.*
"Tell him no more."
*He does not think. It is I who must think.*
"Did you think to kill this child,
whose remains I remove from your womb?"
You grab at her hand again
desperation raging.

She must know
that you cannot do this again
that eight is more than you can afford
that your eldest is with child
that your youngest has no milk
and you have no love left for anyone.

"*Theek hai, theek hai,* alright, alright
Let me do my work," she shakes her head
with the understanding
of a woman.

# Box of Treasures

As a child I stored my treasures
in an old Black Magic tin
a girl guide badge
fancy buttons
a brooch with missing stones
and other precious silly things.

One of my favourite pastimes
was to take my box to a quiet place
and rummage through its contents
delighting in my treasures.

Today, I have a house filled with treasures
too numerous to list
too busy to delight in.

# Girl

She walks along the backroad of life
treading timidly
giving way to all others
mistress of nothing
no claim to land or name
her identity drawn and overshadowed
by every male in her life
daughter of her father
wife of her husband
mother of her son.

She walks along the backroad
invisible
her footsteps make no sound
on the concrete tract of ideology
and leave no imprint
in the shifting sands of time

*Author's note: referencing the plight of the girl-child in some cultures*

# Soul Sister

*for Rosemary*

Chance meeting in a busy place,
your soul reached out to touch me
and kindred spirits met.

Words flew between us
found commonality in diverse realities,
two strangers like long-lost friends
gloried in the bonding.

We parted, glancing back at each other,
flushed with the knowledge of soul-kinship,
not knowing it would be our only meeting.

My dear friend, I remember that day often.
I think of you, a beautiful spirit,
bright, wise, full of joy.
I think of the journals that you spoke of
filled with reflections of a life well-savoured,
perhaps a lost legacy.

# I am Home

Clenched fists pound air.
Rage of the mob pierces the TV screen,
spills hatred, venom
into our family room,
making us uneasy.

Bearded men in turbans
surge through streets
I once walked on
claiming to speak for the nation
I once belonged to.
I see madness in the eyes and think
this is not me.
Only a few women in sight
are shrouded in cultural dogmas.
This is not me either.

*Ingrate!* Conscience admonishes,
*You once thrived on that land.*
    It was different then, I object.
    Things have changed. I have changed.

*Look at the face of Canada? Is this you?*
    I see diversity. I see freedom.
    Yes, this *is* me.
    I am home.

*Write a poem, children*
*begin with "I love Canada, because…"*

# I Love Canada, Because...

*Write a poem, children*
begin with *"I love Canada, because…"*

Bright-eyes blink,
little heads lock conspiratorially,
little scribes dig lead into paper,
swish erasers, whisk off first thoughts.

*Would you like to read your poem?*
Eager hands shoot up.

Hockey and maple syrup,
the Ex and Wonderland,
spelled every which way
on every list,
pizza and burgers, tacos and sushi.

Pure gems of connection as in
fishing with *grandpere,*
*amma's* roti,
*nonna's* cannoli.

Free verse took flight
finding and losing rhyme.

Tender beginnings of
*"I love Canada, because..."*

# Small Iniquity

*"God sees your iniquity – even before you commit it."*
My pre-teen mind balked at big words
that added mystery to the Great Mystery.
It was not fear of God or Lucifer
that took me to the confession box.
Between parent and priest
there was never an option.

I peer at the silhouette behind the screened window.
Does he really stand in for God?
He, who had caned the boys in front of the girls
just to prove his power?
Did he recognize me on this side of the screen
as I did him?

I never tell him my real sins,
just repeat the sample ones I learned in catechism.
Confession boxes are stifling hot like hell.
Guilt trickles down my neck,
soaks the collar of my polyester dress.
My hand in my pocket clutches the four annas
meant for the collection box.
It was enough for two pieces of fudge
from Vellozo's snack shop.

# The Little Red Streamer

Years ago, I turned on the ceiling fan and a wisp of red crepe-paper streamer, leftover from Christmas, began a slow circle above, waved in the fan's motion, "Look at me! I am here! Remember the fun and festivity?" Then the fan, picked up speed, and frantically whirled around in a blur.

Today, an ocean away, I delight in recreating Christmases past in true Goan tradition: new clothes for the season, tedious-to-make-cholesterol-fat-sugar-packed homemade confections. I hope to pass on the joy of that wonderful memory to my kids and keep the tradition alive.

However, my husband and I are generally alone making the sweets, consulting our precious, well-used Goan recipe book. On big days, turkey and trimmings sit beside *sorportel* and *sannas*, the former disappearing faster than the latter.

"Mum, do you know 'sop-a-tell' has organ meat, packed with cholesterol—so like, not good for you and Dad?" Followed by the totally demoralizing: "Don't cook it before my friends come over."

The sense of obligation to pass on traditions and good memories of Christmases past gets less duty-bound as the years go by. And the strong energy and digestion involved in upholding them grows lesser and lesser as well.

"This is how we did it! It was such a grand time! Really. It was! A Grand Time!"

I feel the angst of a forlorn wisp of red streamer waving and whirling on the ceiling fan.

# A Prayer

Dear Lord,

Thank you for the gift of Muse,
for guiding me to the inspirational works
of others who influenced and guided
my own journey to self-empowerment.

Thank you for helping me
weather storms and parched times
and rejoice in fine days.

Thank you for the strength
to make the shift from fear to joy,
from victim to survivor,
for opening alternative pathways
on my journey to self-fulfillment
in a life of true purpose.

May I inspire others
as I have been inspired by others.

Thank you for all I have and receive.

Thank you, Lord.

# Reviews for 'Bruised but Unbroken'

With heart-aching resonance and a forthrightness that cannot but move you, Antao-Xavier returns to the past, reconciles old and new selves, and finds comfort in the present. I see in her, and in her poetry, a kindred 'unbroken spirit,' who lives life with devotion and humility, courage and truth, sadness and joy, and with a desire to serve.

*--Dr. Ranjini George, Professor and author of* Through My Mother's Window: Emirati Women Tell Their Stories and Recipes.

In a time where women have been forced to assemble worldwide to defend their rights, the re-emergence of *Bruised but Unbroken* is both timely and necessary. Antao-Xavier portrays the female experience in smooth and compelling lines. *--Brandon Pitts, author,* Pressure to Sing, Tender in the Age of Fury, *and* In the Company of Crows.

Cheryl's words feel like a beacon, lighting the way for the reader and ultimately delivering them through their own brokenness. The sprinkling of haikus throughout her book provides a refreshing touch, like that of a gentle shower of hope. The strength in her prose creates a restorative power that is palpable. *--Susan Ksiezopolski, author of* My Words, Writing for Change *and* The Writer's Workshop.

*Bruised but Unbroken* is a personal, in-your-face collection of poetry that focuses on the theme of not giving up, of overcoming, of reflecting on what's been done to you or your loved ones and taking a stand. I loved it. Great poetry is moving. It is personal and philosophical, and shines light on our hidden hopes and secret despairs. Antao-Xavier's collection does exactly that.- *-Adam Fernandes, writer, educationist, activist, adam-fernandes.blogspot.ca.*

Cheryl Antao-Xavier's new collection is 'a box of treasures.' Each poem is a prayer of faith in our own spirit, inviting us to forge ahead in spite of obstacles, to 'step out of the margins' and lift our soul 'out of misfortune, healed and unbroken.' *--Josie Di Sciascio-Andrews, teacher, poet & author of* Letters from the Singularity *and* Jar of Fireflies, *Host & Coordinator of the Oakville Literary Café.*

This is poetry at its powerful best: digging deep to wring out unspoken thoughts from the depths of the soul. Frustration, despair, heartbreak all simmer through, then pour out in the form of words that often leave you gasping at the rawness of emotion. *Bruised but Unbroken* is not just poetry that will have you marvelling at the unquestionable skill of its author, its emotional undercurrent will touch your heart.

*--Archie D'Cruz, publisher, atypeofmagic.com.*

Cheryl's work is honest and from the heart. She takes you up to the edge of a clear pond and makes absolutely no apology for pushing you right in along with her. As you swim in her words, her colours and her experiences, you break the surface knowing that you have merged with the flow of all life, finding the similarity in being alive.

*--Susan Munro, mystic poet; esoteric/alternative healer, author of* Coil *and* Ravings of a Lunatic Saint.

Cheryl Antao-Xavier's heartfelt poetry gently lights up the pages with well-crafted verses spanning moments and years.

*--I.B. Iskov, Founder, The Ontario Poetry Society.*

*Bruised but Unbroken* breathes life into women's empowerment by exposing the grim truth of oppression and the culpability of complacency therein.

*--Jasmine Jackman, educator, author, motivator.*

Cheryl writes from the heart, which is why her poetry is deeply touching. She has the unique ability of using words like a paintbrush...The final picture is a work of art.

*--KumKum Ramchandani, artist, poet, author of* Bailey's Blogs.

The resilience of the human spirit is so evocatively expressed in Cheryl's poems. Each poem is a pearl, born of an irritant speck of dust, of negativity that over time finds acceptance of a new self, new strength and burnished by experience, transforms into a lustrous bead.

*--Geeta Krishnamoorthy, part-time poet.*

We women find ourselves at a point where our inner development demands a proportionate degree of respect and influence in society. As we discover the dignity in us and as we live it, we can no longer compromise, instead we now demand to see it reflected in the family, society and the world. *--Lilly Tadin, President, Women's Federation for World Peace, Canada; Vice-President, WFWP International.*

Antao-Xavier shows in stark reality the abuse of women and injustices at the hands of a male-dominated society. Inner afflictions are magnified via powerful images that touch the heart and soul of the reader. *--Maria Pia Marchelletta, multilingual poet; editor; artist; President, Writers & Editors Network, Toronto.*

*Bruised but Unbroken* is brilliantly crafted, a testimony to the resiliency of women to 'rise again.' Cheryl Xavier portrays lived experiences that create empowering mindfulness and healing, which disrupts the transmission of intergenerational violence. A must read for all who resist social inequities and human rights violations. *--Rita Kohli, feminist, writer, human rights activist.*

Cheryl's candid depiction of the harsh realities of life is balanced with the conveyance of our Spirit's enduring resilience. Her words are catalytic, bringing awareness to how perspective changes insurmountable barriers to growth and inner strength. She grounds one to live in the present moment with gratitude. *--Lindsay W. Albert, poet, author of* One Life—Different Perspectives.

www.ingramcontent.com/pod-product-compliance
Ingram Content Group UK Ltd.
Pitfield, Milton Keynes, MK11 3LW, UK
UKHW020422250726
13967UKWH00007B/2775